ONE DAY AT DISNEY

A ROUNDTABLE PRESS BOOK

A Roundtable Press Book

New York

For Hyperion
Editor: Wendy Lefkon
Assistant Editor: Rich Thomas

For Roundtable Press, Inc.
Directors: Susan E. Meyer, Marsha Melnick, Julie Merberg
Art Director: Nai Chang
Production Editor: John Glenn
Text: Pam Brandon
Design and computer production: Steven Rosen

ISBN 0-7868-6592-X

First Edition
2 4 6 8 10 9 7 5 3 1

OPPOSITE:
WALT DISNEY WORLD, FLORIDA,
4:32 P.M.
Makinzie Grimmer from Holt, Michigan,
sprints across the Magic Kingdom Walk of
Fame located just outside the theme park.

C O N T

E N T S

INTRODUCTION

With four Disney theme parks on three continents—Disneyland in California, the Walt Disney World Resort in Florida, Tokyo Disneyland in Japan, and Disneyland Paris in France—you could literally jet around the world and still be able to walk through the open gates of one of the four parks. The sun never sets on the magic, for when it is closing time in Florida, halfway around the world in Japan the theme park is just opening for another day.

This global wonder all started with Walt Disney's dream to create a three-dimensional extension of his hugely successful animated films. But it also was a special gift to his own children. "Disneyland came about," he said in the early 1950s, "when my daughters were very young and Saturday was always daddy's day. It all started from a daddy with two daughters wondering where he could take them and where he could have a little fun with them, too."

Simple pleasures, it seems, that became so much more as Walt engaged his favorite animators in creating Disneyland, "seen through the eyes of my imagination—a place of warmth and nostalgia, of illusion and color and delight," he explained.

The dream became reality when Disneyland opened to the public in July of 1955. "We are just getting started," he said, not truly knowing what a prescient statement that was.

And how surprised he would be to see what his dream has become! Walt only lived to see California Disneyland, but his ideas of reaching out to the rest of the world were coming to life when he broke ground for the second park, Walt Disney World Resort near Orlando, Florida. That theme park opened in October 1971, followed by Tokyo Disneyland in April 1983, and Disneyland Paris in April 1992.

Although millions of guests travel every year to these magical places, it is unusual for anyone to have the opportunity to visit all four parks on three continents. And because the Disney experience appears to be seamless, there has always been a tremendous curiosity about what happens when the gates are closed, or backstage before the employees (called cast members), step "onstage" in the parks.

One Day at Disney is a photo album of these four popular theme parks, with images taken over a 24-hour period by sixteen creative photographers. They took nearly three thousand pictures in all, working to show the emotion and the beauty that make the Disney parks truly memorable places. The photos illustrate that the heart of this astonishing business truly lies with the cast members, the people who breathe life into Disney's world of illusion.

We begin our story at closing time—midnight—at Disneyland in California, when it is 3 o'clock in the morning in Florida, 9 o'clock in the morning in France, and 5 o'clock the afternoon in Japan. Stylized clock faces throughout the book illustrate each new hour. When the hands of the clock are white it indicates A.M., black hands indicate P.M. (see below).

Taken all together, the photos in *One Day at Disney* show not only the amazing diversity of guests and of Disney cast members, but most of all they show that the Disney magic transcends time and place—and that a smile is still something everybody, everywhere, expresses in the same language.

"Here you leave today and visit the worlds of yesterday, tomorrow, and fantasy."

– Walt Disney

| MIDNIGHT | 3:00 A.M. | 9:00 A.M. | 5:00 P.M. |
| CALIFORNIA | FLORIDA | PARIS | TOKYO |

ABOVE:
TOKYO DISNEYLAND, 5:45 P.M.
World Bazaar, Tokyo Disneyland's
covered rendition of Main Street,
U.S.A., has a roof to protect it in
inclement weather.

RIGHT:
DISNEYLAND PARIS, 9:00 A.M.
Ready, set, drop! Crowds wait
patiently for the "rope drop"
that signals the official opening in
every Disney park around the
world. Without a second to waste,
fans scurry for their favorite
attractions.

MIDNIGHT
CALIFORNIA

3:00 A.M.
FLORIDA

9:00 A.M.
PARIS

5:00 P.M.
TOKYO

RIGHT:

DISNEYLAND, CALIFORNIA, 12:01 A.M.
Sweet dreams for 3-year-old Digna
Alvarez of Mexico City, who nods off
to sleep as his family heads for home,
just as the theme park is closing.

OPPOSITE TOP:

TOKYO DISNEYLAND, 5:30 P.M.
The soft light of the early evening sky
casts a warm glow on the impressive
façades of the Queen of Hearts
Banquet Hall and It's a Small World.

OPPOSITE, BOTTOM LEFT:

DISNEYLAND PARIS, 9:10 A.M.
On Main Street, U.S.A., shortly after
the opening of Disneyland Paris,
eight-year-old Ambrine Abdulrab of
Mont St. Aignan, France, peeks from
behind her new Minnie Mouse
umbrella.

OPPOSITE, BOTTOM MIDDLE:

DISNEYLAND PARIS, 9:30 A.M.
Waiting is the hard part for brothers
Jeroen and Mienke Elsinga from
Holland, standing in line for Winnie
the Pooh's autograph.

OPPOSITE, BOTTOM RIGHT:

WALT DISNEY WORLD, FLORIDA,
3:20 A.M.
Working on the night shift, Daniel
Shea (left) uses sign language to com-
municate with night-shift co-worker
Gilles Côtè (right). Both are hearing
impaired.

DISNEYLAND PARIS, 9:29 A.M.
The steam train *Eureka* starts its morning journey.
Each day the train carries thousands of guests on
tracks that circle the park.

DISNEYLAND PARIS, 9:48 A.M.
Americana comes to France in
Frontierland aboard the *Mark
Twain Riverboat*, cruising down
the Rivers of the Far West.

TOKYO DISNEYLAND, 5:10 P.M.
A young cast member scoops buckets
of hot popcorn, a favorite fast food
for park guests who are too busy to
stop for lunch.

TOKYO DISNEYLAND, 5:13 P.M. Inspired by the music, 2-year-old Masato Tanaka joins the late afternoon lineup with the Tokyo Disneyland Band.

TOKYO DISNEYLAND, 5:50 P.M. As the day draws to a close, the setting sun casts a warm glow on the Gateway.

DISNEYLAND, CALIFORNIA, 1:30 A.M.
A lone cast member prepares for the thousands of guests who will expect Main Street, U.S.A, to be spotless when they enter the park the next day.

1:00 A.M.
CALIFORNIA

4:00 A.M.
FLORIDA

10:00 A.M.
PARIS

6:00 P.M.
TOKYO

OPPOSITE:
TOKYO DISNEYLAND,
6:00 P.M. - 7:00 P.M.
As twilight turns to night,
Cinderella Castle displays an
ever shifting kaleidescope of colors
and patterns.

RIGHT:
TOKYO DISNEYLAND, 6:34 P.M.
Cultures combine delightfully at
Restaurant Hokusai in World Bazaar,
with staid Victorian storefronts and
delicate Japanese window décor.

TOKYO DISNEYLAND, 6:25 P.M.
Ethereal lighting and sheer curtains of water from the fountain paint a tranquil
picture in the park's picnic area, especially dramatic as night draws near.

TOKYO DISNEYLAND, 6:40 P.M.
Within Fantasyland, the abstract facade of It's a Small World conjures up a fairytale village.

DISNEYLAND PARIS, 10:00 A.M. The photographer took a bird's-eye view of fans awaiting Disney characters who make their grand morning entrance in the lobby of the Disneyland Hotel.

Tokyo Disneyland, 6:35 p.m.
Tinker Bell stands watch as the sunset washes
the sky and creates a surreal effect of
Adventureland icons juxtaposed with
Cinderella Castle.

LEFT:

DISNEYLAND PARIS, 11:05 A.M.
Théo Nestola of Genilac, France, tries with all his might to pull the sword from the stone at Les Miracles d'Excalibur in Fantasyland.

BELOW:

WALT DISNEY WORLD, FLORIDA, 5:59 A.M.
Working just ahead of the early-morning golfers, a groundskeeper repairs the seventh hole on the Palm Course.

2:00 A.M.
CALIFORNIA

5:00 A.M.
FLORIDA

11:00 A.M.
PARIS

7:00 P.M.
TOKYO

ABOVE:

DISNEYLAND PARIS, 11:30 A.M.
The energized cast takes a final bow as the
curtain closes on another successful performance of *Mulan, The Legend* in Videopolis.

RIGHT:

TOKYO DISNEYLAND, 7:30 P.M.
The *Partners* sculpture, portraying Walt Disney
and Mickey Mouse, is illuminated by a blaze
of lights from the Main Street Electrical
Parade.

PREVIOUS PAGE:

TOKYO DISNEYLAND, 7:30 P.M.
Cinderella Castle stands high over the
FANTILLUSION! nighttime spectacular.

RIGHT:

DISNEYLAND, CALIFORNIA, 2:05 A.M.
To keep the brass rails at City Hall shin-
ing, there's no magic: just hours of work
performed on the night shift.

LEFT:

DISNEYLAND PARIS, 11:30 A.M.
In a photograph taken from the Main Street Train Station, the photographer captured a bird's-eye view of young guests in Town Square.

BELOW:

DISNEYLAND PARIS, 11:12 A.M.
Several seamstresses put the finishing touches on a new costume for a cast member at the Hotel New York.

ABOVE:
DISNEYLAND PARIS, 11:15 A.M.
Acrobatics, song, and dance help the animated *Mulan* spring to life in *Mulan, the Legend* at Videopolis.

RIGHT:
DISNEYLAND PARIS, 11:20 A.M.
Meanwhile cast members from the Hebei acrobatic troupe warm up as they wait for their cue to go onstage.

DISNEYLAND PARIS, 11:15 A.M.
Behind the scenes, Frank Hetherton and
Bernard Durand-Rival, architects for
Walt Disney Imagineering, work on a
scale model for City Centre, a future
expansion near Disneyland Paris.

DISNEYLAND, CALIFORNIA, 2:58 A.M.
Balancing on ladders nearly every
night of the year, maintenance work-
ers sand, patch, and paint the miles
of fancy trim works in order to keep
Main Street, U.S.A. looking like new.

 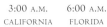

3:00 A.M.   6:00 A.M.   NOON   8:00 P.M.
CALIFORNIA   FLORIDA   PARIS   TOKYO

ABOVE:

DISNEYLAND, CALIFORNIA, 3:17 A.M.
All "streets" inside the attractions need to be swept during the night shift, and this ride track in Alice in Wonderland in Fantasyland is no exception.

LEFT:

WALT DISNEY WORLD, FLORIDA, 6:45 A.M.
The ferry *Richard F. Irvine* moves quietly across the Seven Seas Lagoon to pick up the first Magic Kingdom guests of the day.

ABOVE:
WALT DISNEY WORLD, FLORIDA, 6:30 A.M.
Stars sparkle in the vanishing night sky as
the monorail glides through a silent Epcot
on a pre-opening practice run.

OPPOSITE:
WALT DISNEY WORLD, FLORIDA, 6:53 A.M.
The neon fades, and the natural light of
sunrise paints an entirely different picture
in Tomorrowland.

RIGHT:

WALT DISNEY WORLD,
FLORIDA, 6:12 A.M.
Dawn breaks, and the
"Floral Mickey"
at the entrance to the
Magic Kingdom—a
favorite spot for picture
taking—gets a thorough
dousing to keep it fresh for
the hot Florida sunshine.

OPPOSITE TOP:

WALT DISNEY WORLD,
FLORIDA, 6:30 A.M.
Sunrise paints a primeval
scene in Disney's Animal
Kingdom, where the Tree
of Life spreads its leafy
canopy over the landscape.

OPPOSITE BOTTOM:

WALT DISNEY WORLD,
FLORIDA, 6:40 A.M.
Moments later, the sun
lightens the clouds and a
work crew floats down
Discovery River, beginning
the work day.

TOKYO DISNEYLAND, 8:05 P.M. All the Disney characters must be asleep in wacky Toontown, where the exaggerated details are even more striking after dark.

TOKYO DISNEYLAND, 8:20 P.M. The splash of Roger Rabbit's Fountain is the only sound in the quiet streets of Toontown.

WALT DISNEY WORLD, FLORIDA,
6:40 A.M.
Mickey Mouse begins another
day, surveying his kingdom from
the portal of Cinderella Castle.

DISNEYLAND PARIS, NOON
Cinderella's Golden Carriage catches the eye of
hungry guests searching for fine dining in
Auberge de Cendrillon (Cinderella's Inn), a
restaurant in Fantasyland.

DISNEYLAND PARIS, 12:20 P.M. Cast members take a break backstage at the refueling station for the Autopia raceway attraction, while a colorful performance of the parade, *Mulan, la Célébration d'une Légende,* takes place in the park's Central Plaza.

WALT DISNEY WORLD, FLORIDA, 7:30 A.M.
In the peaceful early morning fog, cast member Ryan Seay gives Central Plaza a final sweep before the park opens.

DISNEYLAND, CALIFORNIA, 4:15 A.M.
The frenzied character from *Mulan* is merely part of the décor in the Emporium, where an artist puts finishing touches on the varnished floor.

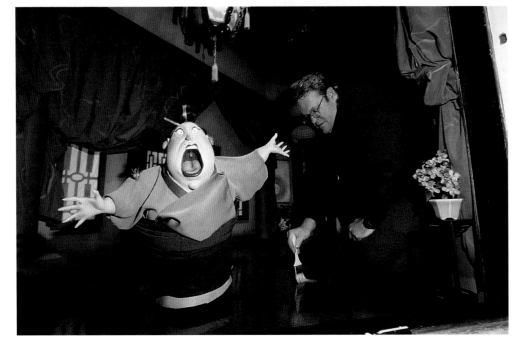

4:00 A.M.
CALIFORNIA

7:00 A.M.
FLORIDA

1:00 P.M.
PARIS

9:00 P.M.
TOKYO

DISNEYLAND PARIS, 1:05 P.M.
Outside Phantom Manor, a couple of
Minnie balloons tethered to strollers
share a light-as-air moment.

LEFT:
DISNEYLAND PARIS, 1:40 P.M.
A crisp spring day and a
waterfall are the right
ingredients for Severine
and Nicolas, who find a
moment for romance at
Skull Rock in Adventureland.

OPPOSITE, TOP:
WALT DISNEY WORLD,
FLORIDA, 7:30 A.M.
Shortly after sunrise, giraffes
take a stroll down the ride
path for Kilimanjaro Safaris
at Disney's Animal Kingdom.

OPPOSITE, BOTTOM:
WALT DISNEY WORLD,
FLORIDA, 7:45 A.M.
A curious female ostrich
awakens to survey the
savannah at Disney's Animal
Kingdom, where a diverse
population of creatures
roams freely.

TOP LEFT:
TOKYO DISNEYLAND, 9:00 P.M. Now that the last diners have departed from Restaurant Hokusai, this cast member puts the finishing touches on the end of her day.

BOTTOM LEFT:
DISNEYLAND PARIS, 1:10 P.M. Two cast members share a light moment over lunch backstage in the Main Street Cafeteria before heading off to work.

OPPOSITE:
WALT DISNEY WORLD, FLORIDA, 7:20 A.M. Engineer Andy Leonard, 75, has worked on the Walt Disney World steam trains since 1976, and pal Roy Langsdon, 69, a retired minister, has been a conductor for twelve years.

47

DISNEYLAND, CALIFORNIA, 4:05 A.M.
A tiny brush, a steady hand, and
plenty of patience are needed when
it is time to touch up the signs on
the Main Street, U.S.A. Camera Shop.

WALT DISNEY WORLD, FLORIDA, 7:25 A.M.
The neat and tidy rows of tables and chairs soon will be askew at the popular Plaza Restaurant on Main Street, U.S.A.

LEFT:
DISNEYLAND PARIS, 2:44 P.M.
A smiling Pierre-Henri Feurion, just moments before he heads onstage in the Wonderful World of Disney Parade.

OPPOSITE, TOP LEFT:
DISNEYLAND PARIS, 2:45 P.M.
A chivalrous performer laces a friend's shoes as they get into costume for the parade floats.

OPPOSITE, TOP RIGHT:
WALT DISNEY WORLD, FLORIDA, 8:15 A.M.
Fireworks technician Dave Murphy loads explosives into launch tubes for the nightly fireworks.

OPPOSITE, MIDDLE ROW:
DISNEYLAND PARIS, 2:30 P.M.
In the backstage workshop, designers complete last-minute work and issue costumes for the Wonderful World of Disney Parade.

OPPOSITE, BOTTOM ROW:
WALT DISNEY WORLD, FLORIDA, 8:07 A.M.
Cast member Isle Voght works on the renovation of a carrousel chariot that will be added to Cinderella's Golden Carrousel in the Magic Kingdom.

5:00 A.M.
CALIFORNIA

8:00 A.M.
FLORIDA

2:00 P.M.
PARIS

10:00 P.M.
TOKYO

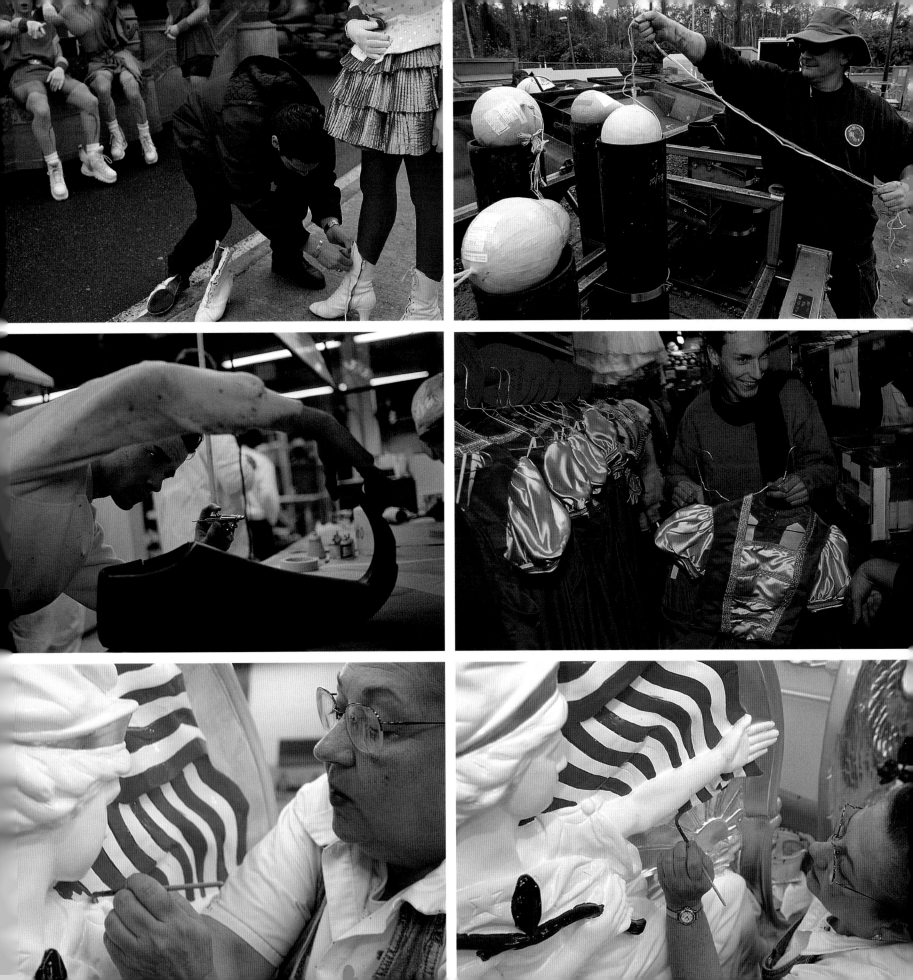

OPPOSITE:

TOKYO DISNEYLAND, 10:15 P.M.
"Take me home!" Mickey Mouse pleads with a smile and outstretched arms in a merchandise display in World Bazaar.

TOP:

DISNEYLAND PARIS, 2:30 P.M.
A spirited makeup artist puts the final touches on the clowns for the Dumbo float in the Wonderful World of Disney Parade.

ABOVE:

DISNEYLAND PARIS, 2:10 P.M.
A guest wraps up and settles in her front-row seat as she waits for the afternoon parade.

TOKYO DISNEYLAND, 10:10 P.M.
Under nighttime skies, Tomorrowland looks like a
giant science-fantasy community of the future.

DISNEYLAND, CALIFORNIA, 5:30 A.M.
It may look like an authentic Wild West trading
post, but there are lightbulbs to be changed before
the morning shoppers arrive at Buffalo Traders.

DISNEYLAND, CALIFORNIA,
5:45 A.M.
As day breaks, a landscaper in a miner's helmet starts to mow the lawn for a perfect cut in front of Sleeping Beauty Castle.

WALT DISNEY WORLD, FLORIDA, 8:30 A.M. Horticulturist Sam Sheperd trims the topiary at the Walt Disney World Tree Farm. Every day, hundreds of gardeners at the 190-acre Tree Farm tend thousands of plants, trees, shrubs, and flowers for use throughout Walt Disney World Resort.

DISNEYLAND PARIS, 3:30 P.M.
It's the moment of a lifetime for
young Manon Meunier from
Dijon, France.

6:00 A.M.
CALIFORNIA

9:00 A.M.
FLORIDA

3:00 P.M.
PARIS

11:00 P.M.
TOKYO

WALT DISNEY WORLD, FLORIDA, 9:30 AM.
An assortment of favorite Disney friends—the
plush versions—make the trek home with a family
camping at Disney's Fort Wilderness Resort.

DISNEYLAND PARIS, 3:30 P.M.
"Some Day My Prince Will Come"… perhaps on a
steam locomotive? Megan Ramsay and Louise Allen,
girlhood friends on holiday from England, share
secrets as they wait at Discoveryland Station.

DISNEYLAND, CALIFORNIA, 6:40 A.M.
The monorail pilot backs out of the roundhouse to start the daily circuit.

DISNEYLAND PARIS, 3:30 P.M.
An afternoon view from the Town Square gazebo of
Le Château de la Belle au Bois Dormant, or Sleeping
Beauty Castle.

BELOW:

WALT DISNEY WORLD, FLORIDA, 9:05 A.M.
It's not a posse, but the first guests of the day,
escorted by cast members to Frontierland attractions
in the Magic Kingdom.

DISNEYLAND PARIS, 3:07 P.M.
Fantasy creatures from *Hercules* tower over the crowds
lining Main Street, U.S.A., for the Wonderful
World of Disney Parade.

WALT DISNEY WORLD, FLORIDA, 9:02 A.M.
And they're off! Moments after the park opens,
crowds of excited guests rush through the Main
Street, U.S.A train station, each hoping to be first in
line at their favorite attraction.

DISNEYLAND, CALIFORNIA,
6:45 A.M.
Cast members are already at work before the theme park opens. The paint will barely have time to dry before the first guests begin to stroll down Main Street, U.S.A. Meanwhile, the streets of Frontierland become an early-morning staging area as new merchandise is unloaded.

RIGHT:
DISNEYLAND, CALIFORNIA, 7:05 A.M.
The churro wagon gets an early-morning tow into Frontierland.

RIGHT AND BOTTOM RIGHT:
DISNEYLAND PARIS, 4:30 P.M.
With a retro design inspired by the views of 19th-century visionaries like Jules Verne and H.G. Wells, Space Mountain in Discoveryland hurtles passengers through a starry cosmos. And as the countdown commences, an apprehensive guest takes a last look before blast-off.

7:00 A.M.
CALIFORNIA

10:00 A.M.
FLORIDA

4:00 P.M.
PARIS

MIDNIGHT
TOKYO

DISNEYLAND PARIS, 4:40 P.M.
Two youngsters set off on a
late-afternoon escapade in
Adventureland, seemingly
unaware of their unusual view
of Le Château de la Belle au
Bois Dormant (Sleeping
Beauty Castle).

DISNEYLAND PARIS, 4:50 P.M.
The pastel facade of It's a Small World softens
against a brilliant blue late-afternoon sky.

DISNEYLAND PARIS, 4:05 P.M.
In a surprising juxtaposition of scale, the giant open
storybook stands near the miniature buildings in Le
Pays des Contes de Fées (The Land of Fairytales).

OPPOSITE:
WALT DISNEY WORLD,
FLORIDA, 10:10 A.M.
Children love the gentle flight
above Fantasyland on Dumbo
the Flying Elephant, one of
the most popular Disney
attractions of all time.

RIGHT:
WALT DISNEY WORLD,
FLORIDA, 10:12 A.M.
A musician since he was 10
years old, sousaphone player
Ed Firth, now age 47, has per-
formed with the Walt Disney
World Band for 16 years.

DISNEYLAND PARIS, 4:50 P.M.
A re-creation of the
Hyperion airship from the
film *The Island at the Top of the
World* floats over the entrance
to Videopolis.

DISNEYLAND PARIS, 4:10 P.M. It's not fog but manufactured steam that creates the ambience of America's red rock country at Big Thunder Mountain Railroad.

TOP LEFT:
WALT DISNEY WORLD, FLORIDA,
11:15 A.M.
Minnie Mouse joins in an impromptu mid-morning family portrait at the Disney-MGM Studios. The brothers and sisters have come to Florida from their home in Lake Jackson, Texas.

BOTTOM LEFT AND OPPOSITE:
DISNEYLAND PARIS, 5:12 P.M.
All good things must come to an end. The magic gets packed away for the long drive home to the Dordogne, France, while a family waits for the train at the TGV station just outside the entrance to the theme park.

8:00 A.M.   11:00 A.M.   5:00 P.M.   1:00 A.M.
CALIFORNIA   FLORIDA   PARIS   TOKYO

DISNEYLAND PARIS, 5:05 P.M.
The early-evening sunlight paints a picture of exotic,
faraway places. The warm colors and distinctive
Arabian shapes in Adventureland evoke the spirit of
the animated film *Aladdin*.

TOKYO DISNEYLAND, 1:10 A.M.
The photographer has captured, high atop the
Crystal Palace, a lone cast member, who is cleaning
each window in the luminous restaurant by hand.

LEFT:

DISNEYLAND, CALIFORNIA, 8:30 A.M.
The flowers get a final drink of water just minutes before guests start streaming down Main Street, U.S.A.

ABOVE:

WALT DISNEY WORLD, FLORIDA, 11:05 A.M.
A cast member dives right into this giant bucket of water. It just so happens that the water is actually made of fiberglass and he is hard at work, finishing the gargantuan props for the *Fantasia* area at Disney's All-Star Movies Resort.

DISNEYLAND, CALIFORNIA, 8:40 A.M.

Minutes before the official opening of the park, cast members gather to honor one of their own. Retiring Disneyland photographer and archivist Renié Bardeau receives the greatest tribute bestowed upon a Disney cast member: his own window "advertisement" on Main Street, U.S.A. The window is in place overhead; Renié gets his own copy to keep.

TOKYO DISNEYLAND, 1:33 A.M.
The deserted streets of World
Bazaar glisten like ice after they
are washed.

DISNEYLAND, CALIFORNIA, 9:00 A.M.
A young guest gets the honor of helping a cast member with the official morning opening, but when the rope drops, the crowd just wants to bolt immediately for favorite attractions.

| 9:00 A.M. | NOON | 6:00 P.M. | 2:00 A.M. |
| CALIFORNIA | FLORIDA | PARIS | TOKYO |

DISNEYLAND PARIS, 6:12 P.M.
After receiving some touch-ups, the setting from
Disney's The Hunchback of Notre Dame—a Musical Adventure
gets towed back to the stage.

DISNEYLAND PARIS, 6:18 P.M.
The photographer has taken an unusual view of Le Château de la Belle au Bois Dormant (Sleeping Beauty Castle) through the giant leaves in Alice's Curious Labyrinth in Fantasyland.

ABOVE:

WALT DISNEY WORLD, FLORIDA, NOON
Those fuzzy yellow arms belong to Winnie the Pooh, snuggling with
Emma Levin of Moorestown, New Jersey at the Disney-MGM Studios.

RIGHT:

DISNEYLAND PARIS, 6:36 P.M.
It's been a day to remember for this satisfied young guest, departing for
London from the Disneyland train station.

LEFT:
WALT DISNEY WORLD, FLORIDA, 12:32 P.M.
Like spectators vying for space, shiny
Mickey and Minnie balloons keep a noon-
day watch over Main Street, U.S.A.

BELOW:
WALT DISNEY WORLD, FLORIDA, NOON
There's no mistaking where you are when
arriving in the land of Mickey Mouse; even
the street poles sport mouse ears.

DISNEYLAND PARIS, 7:38 P.M.
All aglow except for one burned-out bulb, cast member Steve Lowe gets a quick fix before heading onstage for the night's performance of the Main Street Electrical Parade.

10:00 A.M.
CALIFORNIA

1:00 P.M.
FLORIDA

7:00 P.M.
PARIS

3:00 A.M.
TOKYO

LEFT:

WALT DISNEY WORLD, FLORIDA, 1:46 P.M.
Megan Chiong keeps a comforting arm around
1-year-old Paulina Kuo as the irrepressible Tigger
embraces them both at the Disney-MGM Studios.

BELOW:

WALT DISNEY WORLD, FLORIDA, 1:30 P.M.
Four-year-old Ethan Ellwood from England gives
his opponent a thorough dousing from an unusual
water cannon located at River Country water park
at Disney's Fort Wilderness Resort.

DISNEYLAND, CALIFORNIA, 10:22 A.M.
From behind the Mad Hatter of *Alice in Wonderland*,
the photographer takes an inclusive view of the
mornings activities. While the Disneyland Band is
playing around them, Alice gathers some friends to
enjoy a wacky game with him in the Castle
Forecourt.

DISNEYLAND, CALIFORNIA, 10:02 A.M.
Minnie Mouse and Pluto catch a
morning ride in an old-fashioned jit-
ney down Main Street, U.S.A.

TOKYO DISNEYLAND, 3:00 A.M. Imagine a scene from a sci-fi film, with an alien slithering from underground. Odd, isn't it, that this image is actually the equipment used by the night crew in Tomorrowland?

TOKYO DISNEYLAND, 3:14 A.M.
Walking through the park, the photographer takes
notice of the cast members and their chores. Here,
World Bazaar is getting its nightly hose-down.

TOKYO DISNEYLAND, 3:34 A.M.
Here the photographer finds a cast member using an extension pole to retrieve an errant helium balloon from a building.

DISNEYLAND PARIS, 7:20 P.M. It may look like a scene from days of yore, but in the modern-day version the vendor is selling personalized blocks to pave Promenade Disney, and the castle behind is the Disneyland Hotel.

DISNEYLAND, CALIFORNIA, 11:25 A.M.
What better way to cool off in the
midday heat than dodging the spouting waters of the interactive fountains
in Tomorrowland?

11:00 A.M.
CALIFORNIA

2:00 P.M.
FLORIDA

8:00 P.M.
PARIS

4:00 A.M.
TOKYO

WALT DISNEY WORLD, FLORIDA, 2:30 P.M.
The photographer has captured the special moment
millions of children dream of—a hug from the Big
Cheese himself.

WALT DISNEY WORLD, FLORIDA, 2:32 P.M.
A flock of bright Mickey Mouse balloons creates a
colorful snapshot on Main Street, U.S.A.

TOKYO DISNEYLAND, 4:30 A.M. Finishing up just before daybreak, a cast member rewinds a giant spool of water hose.

DISNEYLAND PARIS, 8:35 P.M. Behind the scenes, sharing a light moment with his colleagues, this cast member gets into costume for Buffalo Bill's Wild West Show.

ABOVE:

WALT DISNEY WORLD, FLORIDA, 2:18 P.M.
Boatswain mates Albert Viray and Rodrigo
Santoyo give Goofy a scrub as part of the daily
maintenance aboard *Disney Magic,* the first ship
for the Disney Cruise Line. Goofy is always
hanging off the stern, a perfect addition to the
ship's whimsical décor.

RIGHT:

WALT DISNEY WORLD, FLORIDA, 2:12 P.M.
A view of the monorail and Spaceship Earth
from the west side of Future World.

DISNEYLAND PARIS, 9:20 P.M.
At Buffalo Bill's Wild West Show, sturdy appaloosas gallop at lightning speed in the arena, demonstrating the great skills of the horsemen riding them.

DISNEYLAND, PARIS, 9:01 PM.
A ten-gallon hat is a tad too big for this little cowpoke at the souvenir photo location at Buffalo Bill's Wild West Show.

NOON
CALIFORNIA

3:00 P.M.
FLORIDA

9:00 P.M.
PARIS

5:00 A.M.
TOKYO

DISNEYLAND, CALIFORNIA, 12:02 P.M.
At any time of day the famous *Partners* sculpture of
Walt Disney and Mickey Mouse, with Sleeping
Beauty Castle as a backdrop, is one of the most
photographed views in Disneyland.

DISNEYLAND PARIS, 9:15 P.M.
The enormous reflecting pool at the Hotel New York, called the Central Park Fountain, becomes an ice-skating rink in the winter, inspired by the real thing at Rockefeller Plaza in New York City.

DISNEYLAND, CALIFORNIA,
NOON
The hustle and bustle of
happy crowds, the clip clop
of horse-drawn trolleys,
and the festive spires of
Sleeping Beauty Castle all
combine to form a scene of
joyful activity along Main
Street, U.S.A.

WALT DISNEY WORLD,
FLORIDA, 3:20 P.M.
Every day in the Magic
Kingdom, children are
thrilled to see their favorite
characters go by during the
afternoon parade. Here,
perched on his father's shoul-
ders, 3-year-old Davis
Roethler of St. Louis stares
up at the genie from *Aladdin*
and makes a wish. But was it
granted? Only Davis knows
for sure.

TOKYO DISNEYLAND, 5:46 A.M.
A bucket of soapsuds sits incongru-
ously after sunrise in the middle of
Westernland.

ABOVE:

TOKYO DISNEYLAND, 6:05 A.M.
An artist touches up the exaggerated
architectural details on the surface of
one of the buildings in Toontown.

OPPOSITE:

TOKYO DISNEYLAND, 6:45 A.M.
The dolls in It's a Small World—
there are nearly 300 in all—get a
sprucing up from the overnight crew.

1:00 P.M.　　4:00 P.M.　　10:00 P.M.　　6:00 A.M.
CALIFORNIA　　FLORIDA　　PARIS　　TOKYO

ABOVE:
DISNEYLAND PARIS, 10:11 P.M.
A pleasantly exhausted Samantha Fathers, on holiday from London, catnaps in the lobby of the Sequoia Lodge after a full day of activity.

RIGHT:
DISNEYLAND PARIS, 10:30 P.M.
The curtain opens for Minnie Mouse's final bow at the Lucky Nugget Saloon show in Frontierland.

DISNEYLAND, CALIFORNIA,
1:50 P.M.
A new coat of paint is
added to a giant alligator
float at the Parade Building.

Located behind Frontierland
and Fantasyland is an area
known as the Circle D
Corral, home to all the non-
human cast members in
Disneyland. The tenants are
mainly horses and ponies, but
occasionally another species
takes up residence. For
instance, here, a dauntless
animal trainer affectionately
handles a python.

LEFT:
WALT DISNEY WORLD,
FLORIDA, 4:05 P.M.
Magic Kingdom balloon
hostess Dana Bateman seems
lost in a swirl of color.

OPPOSITE:
WALT DISNEY WORLD,
FLORIDA, 4:50 P.M.
An officer aboard the *Disney
Magic* checks on the release
of the dock lines as the ship
prepares for departure from
Port Canaveral, Florida.

HOTEL NEW YORK

OPPOSITE:
DISNEYLAND PARIS, 10:51 P.M.
The Hotel New York, designed by
renowned architect Michael Graves,
recalls America of the late 1920s
and 1930s as it looked at the height
of the Art Deco craze.

RIGHT:
WALT DISNEY WORLD, FLORIDA,
5:45 P.M.
A peaceful scene in the moat sur-
rounding Cinderella Castle is only
steps away from the bustling crowds
of people on Main Street, U.S.A.

2:00 P.M.   5:00 P.M.   11:00 P.M.   7:00 A.M.
CALIFORNIA   FLORIDA   PARIS   TOKYO

WALT DISNEY WORLD,
FLORIDA 5:20 P.M.
The photographer's lens helps
to lend a sense of scale to the
majestic Tree of Life at
Disney's Animal Kingdom as it
towers 140 feet over the park.
Twenty artists spent 18 months
sculpting the tree, a rich tapes-
try of more than 300 animals,
from the mighty lion to the
playful dolphin.

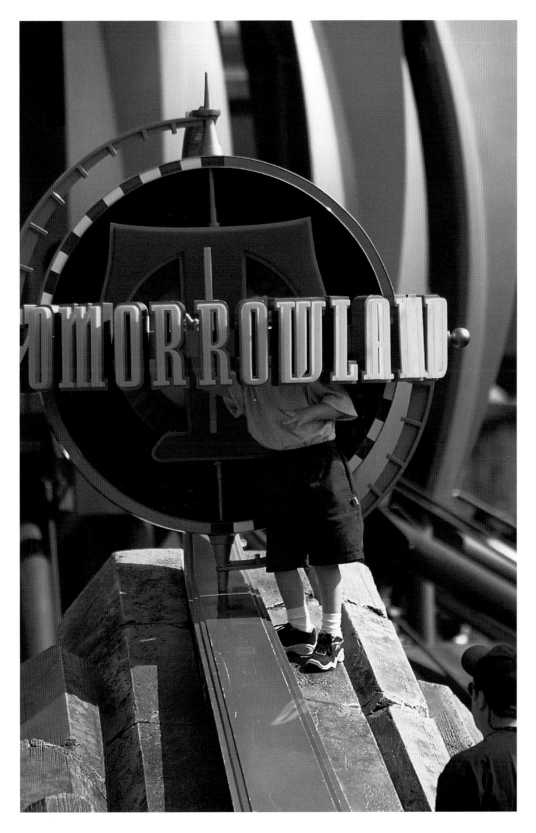

DISNEYLAND, CALIFORNIA, 2:12 P.M.
Forget the attractions: a curious young-ster has plenty of fun just exploring the Tomorrowland sign.

Walt Disney World, Florida, 5:30 p.m.
Music, dance, acrobatics, and elaborate staging and
costuming bring to life the *Festival of the Lion King*,
one of the most talked-about shows at Disney's
Animal Kingdom.

TOKYO DISNEYLAND, 7:08 A.M.
Attention to detail keeps the Disney
parks spotless—even the moat sur-
rounding Cinderella Castle gets an
early-morning scrub, while the trolley
tracks in Toontown get a touch-up.

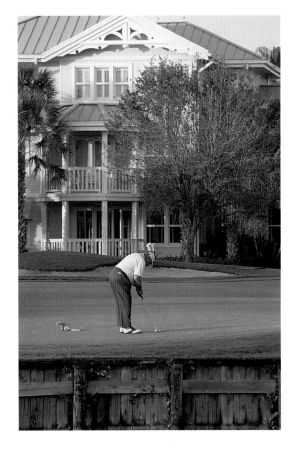

ABOVE:
WALT DISNEY WORLD, FLORIDA, 6:15 P.M.
Late afternoon is the perfect time to hit the
links at the Lake Buena Vista Golf Course
next to Disney's Old Key West Resort.

RIGHT:
TOKYO DISNEYLAND, 8:30 A.M.
Beloved Disney characters make their way to
the main entrance to greet the park's first
visitors of the day.

| 3:00 P.M. | 6:00 P.M. | MIDNIGHT | 8:00 A.M. |
| CALIFORNIA | FLORIDA | PARIS | TOKYO |

TOKYO DISNEYLAND, 8:30 A.M.
The fanciful, ornate buildings and flourishing gardens on the Plaza Terrace suggest the elaborate Victorian architecture of American towns in the late 1800s.

WALT DISNEY WORLD, FLORIDA, 6:49 P.M.
Hollywood Boulevard at the Disney-MGM Studios always gives guests a nostalgic look back at the golden age of Hollywood. This is especially true at sunset when the lights come on and one is overwhelmed with the glitter and glamour that was Tinseltown in the 1930s and 1940s.

TOKYO DISNEYLAND, 8:00 A.M.
Long early-morning shadows stretching
over the Gateway to Tokyo Disneyland
create an inviting pattern for the first
guests of the day.

WALT DISNEY WORLD, FLORIDA, 6:20 P.M.
The soft early-evening light suffuses into pale pastel colors and enhances the feeling of laid-back relaxation at Disney's Old Key West Resort.

DISNEYLAND, CALIFORNIA, 3:35 P.M.
The crowds could be in any busy city, but the outlandish abstract backdrop of It's a Small World is unmistakably Disneyland.

ABOVE:
WALT DISNEY WORLD, FLORIDA, 7:24 P.M.
At the end of a busy day the Adam family, from Chatham, Ontario, gather around the campfire with other guests at Disney's Fort Wilderness Resort for an old-fashioned marshmallow roast.

OPPOSITE:
DISNEYLAND PARIS, 1:55 A.M.
At the Hotel New York, a cast member polishes the big apple, known throughout the world as the quintessential symbol for the American city.

4:00 P.M.
CALIFORNIA

7:00 P.M.
FLORIDA

1:00 A.M.
PARIS

9:00 A.M.
TOKYO

LEFT, TOP ROW:
WALT DISNEY WORLD, FLORIDA,
7:10 P.M.
As daylight fades, the colors of
the sunset create a magical ambience at Cinderella Castle.

LEFT, BOTTOM ROW:
WALT DISNEY WORLD, FLORIDA,
7:35 P.M.
Soon, the sky is a blaze of brilliant pyrotechnics. The festive
finale is a radiant backdrop for
the famed *Partners* sculpture in
front of Cinderella Castle.

137

Tokyo Disneyland,
9:25 A.M.
Minnie Mouse is right at
home in a beautiful hand-
made Japanese dress,
demonstrating the truly
international appeal of
Disney's theme parks.

Tokyo Disneyland, 9:40 a.m.
The world is a different place
when seen from the perspective
of a Disney character, as this
budding Donald Duck discovers.

PREVIOUS PAGE:
DISNEYLAND, CALIFORNIA, 4:03 P.M.
The eccentric architecture of Toontown, where no
right angles are to be found, sparkles in the brilliant
sunlight, providing a bright and colorful environ-
ment for the homes of Mickey, Minnie, Goofy,
Donald, and other cartoon characters.

ABOVE:
DISNEYLAND, CALIFORNIA, 4:20 P.M.
A scene that could be anywhere in the Swiss Alps is
actually located in the heart of Disneyland. The
Matterhorn rises 147 feet, only about 1/100th the
size of its Swiss counterpart.

Tokyo Disneyland, 9:33 a.m.
At the Character Breakfast in the Queen of Hearts
Banquet Hall, 3-year-old Yuto Arai and his big sis-
ter, 5-year-old Ruka, give a big morning hug to
Pinocchio.

OPPOSITE:
TOKYO DISNEYLAND, 10:13 A.M.
A brilliant cloud of balloons fills the morning skies near Cinderella Castle.

TOP RIGHT:
WALT DISNEY WORLD, FLORIDA, 8:45 P.M.
Spaceship Earth, the world's largest geosphere, is an impressive structure, standing 180 feet tall at the entrance to Epcot. Once the sun sets and it's illuminated, it is all the more impressive, resembling a huge sparkling gem.

MIDDLE RIGHT:
DISNEYLAND, CALIFORNIA, 5:36 P.M.
Two-year-old Tabitha Withers of Australia seems somewhat overwhelmed by the likeness of Mickey Mouse created with thousands of flowers at the entrance to Disneyland.

BOTTOM RIGHT:
DISNEYLAND PARIS, 2:38 A.M.
"Wash the dishes, please" takes on a new meaning at the Mad Tea Party attraction in Fantasyland, where the the night crew maintains gargantuan teacups big enough for four grown-ups to sit inside.

| 5:00 P.M. | 8:00 P.M. | 2:00 A.M. | 10:00 A.M. |
| CALIFORNIA | FLORIDA | PARIS | TOKYO |

ABOVE AND OPPOSITE TOP:

TOKYO DISNEYLAND, 10:15 A.M.

During a special parade celebrating the Chinese New Year, East meets West—and a dragon meets Pluto—in a swirling riot of color, sound, and old-fashioned Disney fun.

RIGHT:

TOKYO DISNEYLAND, 10:15 A.M.

As the parade snakes its way through the park, Minnie Mouse and Mickey Mouse give the crowd a special New Year's greeting.

LEFT:

DISNEYLAND, CALIFORNIA, 5:08 P.M.
While the Chinese New Year is being celebrated in
Tokyo, the resplendent Mulan Parade in California
makes its way through the streets of Fantasyland.

DISNEYLAND, CALIFORNIA,
5:05 P.M.
Using the Matterhorn as a
backdrop, this lovely photo-
graph makes Sleeping Beauty
Castle look even more like
Neuschwanstein, the castle in
Bavaria that inspired the
Disneyland version.

DISNEYLAND, CALIFORNIA,
5:11 P.M.
The spires of Space Mountain,
juxtaposed with the brick
facade of Main Street, U.S.A.,
provides an unusual view of
Tomorrowland.

OPPOSITE:

WALT DISNEY WORLD, FLORIDA, 8:01 P.M.
This is an evocative photograph of the replica of Morocco's Nejjarine Fountain. The site showcases the work of 19 artisans who came from Morocco to Florida to work on the World Showcase pavilion at Epcot.

ABOVE:

WALT DISNEY WORLD, FLORIDA, 8:32 P.M.
Shifting from Morocco to Mexico, the photographer has captured the essence of what makes Epcot so unusual. The San Angel Inn restaurant is situated near an ancient Mayan pyramid and a smoky volcano.

OPPOSITE:

DISNEYLAND, CALIFORNIA, 6:31 P.M.
Night falls on Sleeping Beauty Castle.

RIGHT:

TOKYO DISNEYLAND, 11:45 A.M.
Bundled and trundled, brother and
sister Kicka and Yuka Mano, ages 3
and 1, from Chiba, Japan, take in the
sights of Adventureland.

6:00 P.M.   9:00 P.M.   3:00 A.M.   11:00 A.M.
CALIFORNIA   FLORIDA   PARIS   TOKYO

RIGHT:

WALT DISNEY WORLD,
FLORIDA, 9:07 P.M.
A jazz band plays nightly
from the balcony overlook-
ing the opulent lobby of
Disney's Grand Floridian
Resort & Spa.

OPPOSITE TOP:

TOKYO DISNEYLAND,
11:18 A.M.
On the other side of the
world, there is an entirely
different beat: the spicy
rhythms of Latin America
on the Caliente! Caliente!
float in the daily parade.

OPPOSITE BOTTOM:

DISNEYLAND, CALIFORNIA,
6:40 P.M.
In a quiet corner of Main
Street, U.S.A., a cast member passes the time design-
ing watches for guests.

DISNEYLAND, CALIFORNIA, 7:46 P.M.
In each of the Disney theme parks,
throughout the day and evening,
transportation offers a great opportunity for the imagination to take
flight. In California, the *Mark Twain
Riverboat* has been a Disneyland
favorite since 1955. The red rocks of
the thrilling Big Thunder Mountain
Railroad were added in 1979.

7:00 P.M.	10:00 P.M.	4:00 A.M.	NOON
CALIFORNIA	FLORIDA	PARIS	TOKYO

TOKYO DISNEYLAND, NOON
Adventurers journey past exotic sights from the
rivers of the world on the venerable Jungle Cruise.
The amusing safari entertains guests in Tokyo just
as it has in Disneyland, California, since 1955.

WALT DISNEY WORLD,
FLORIDA, 10:25 P.M.
The evening is really just
beginning at Downtown
Disney Pleasure Island as
21-year-old Louis Rodriguez
of New York City shows
off his talents at the BET
Soundstage Club.

WALT DISNEY WORLD,
FLORIDA, 10:55 P.M.
Fire-breathing bartender
George Font not only serves
drinks, but provides bizarre
entertainment at his street-
side bar.

WALT DISNEY WORLD,
FLORIDA, 10:15 P.M.
Tired little legs get a lift
for the walk to the parking
lot after a full day in the
Magic Kingdom Park.

DISNEYLAND, CALIFORNIA,
7:52 P.M.
Tomorrowland's bold sci-fi
architecture glows brilliantly
in the dark.

DISNEYLAND, CALIFORNIA, 7:20 P.M. The Observatron, towering in the background, has been photographed through glowing shoots of water spouting from the fountain in Tomorrowland, creating a scene reminiscent of an army of aliens being beamed down to Earth.

DISNEYLAND,
CALIFORNIA, 7:41 P.M.
At any time of day or
night, the turrets of
Sleeping Beauty Castle
seem to come from the
pages of a fairytale.

TOKYO DISNEYLAND, 1:05 P.M.
Working together every day creates a strong bond of
friendship between Disney cast members, like these
two singers from the Royal Street Six who entertain
at the Royal Street Veranda in Adventureland.

8:00 P.M.	11:00 P.M.	5:00 A.M.	1:00 P.M.
CALIFORNIA	FLORIDA	PARIS	TOKYO

DISNEYLAND PARIS, 5:15 A.M.
Finishing touches are applied to the exterior of a brand new attraction, Honey, I Shrunk the Audience, in Discoveryland.

DISNEYLAND, CALIFORNIA, 8:30 P.M.
Mickey and Minnie escort Cynthia Harris, executive vice president of Disneyland, California, to the stage in order to receive an award in the Grand Ballroom at the Disneyland Hotel.

ABOVE:

TOKYO DISNEYLAND, 1:25 P.M.
Brightly illuminated by a midday sun,
the shady trees and rustic dwellings in
Critter Country are just the right size
to house the rabbits, possums, and
raccoons who are some of the inhabi-
tants of Splash Mountain.

RIGHT:

DISNEYLAND, CALIFORNIA, 8:24 P.M.
The evening meals are in full swing in
Anaheim. Before the night is over
these cooks in the Disneyland Hotel
banquet kitchen will have prepared
hundreds of sweet red peppers for
appetizers.

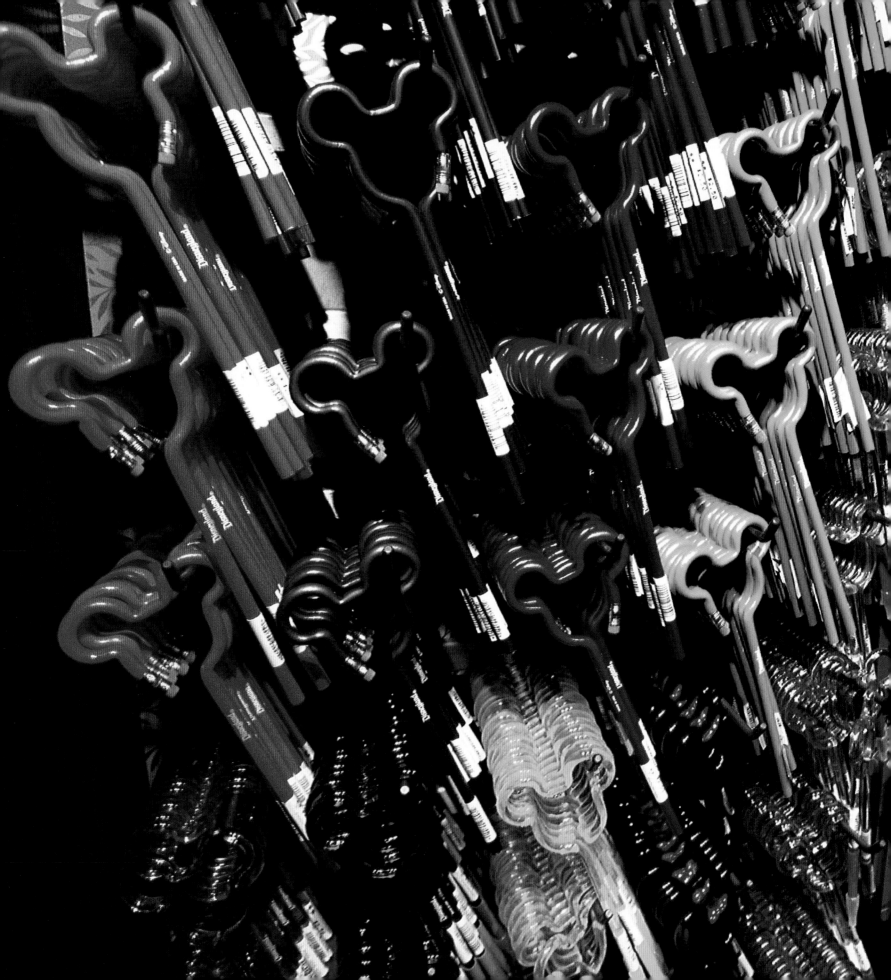

DISNEYLAND, CALIFORNIA, 8:35 P.M.
The photographer was struck by the colorful patterns of Mickey Mouse pencils in this close-up shot in the Emporium on Main Street, U.S.A.

DISNEYLAND, CALIFORNIA, 8:40 P.M.
Across the park in Tomorrowland, shoppers search for just the right keepsake in Star Traders.

WALT DISNEY WORLD, FLORIDA, 12:25 A.M.
It's a wild New Year's Eve celebration every night of
the year at Pleasure Island, and 24-year-old Dario
Diaz of Middletown, New York, is there to party.
As he club hops (opposite), he wows the crowds
along the way. Here, he shows off a handstand at
Mannequins dance club.

9:00 P.M.   MIDNIGHT   6:00 A.M.   2:00 P.M.
CALIFORNIA   FLORIDA   PARIS   TOKYO

TOKYO DISNEYLAND, 2:31 P.M.
One-year-old Riho Hayashi of Kanagawa, Japan,
reluctantly agrees to take an early-afternoon rest on
a bench in Adventureland.

DISNEYLAND PARIS,
6:38 A.M.
The Hotel Santa Fe,
designed by architect
Antoine Predock of New
Mexico, is full of metaphors
about the arid open spaces
of the American West.

TOKYO DISNEYLAND,
2:43 P.M.
The crowd appears to pay
homage to Walt Disney and
Mickey Mouse, but the
guests are actually watching
the daytime Carnivale Parade
as it makes its way past
Cinderella Castle out of the
camera's view.

DISNEYLAND PARIS, 6:20 P.M.
The brilliant red entrance to Disney Village frames
this magical view of the Disneyland Hotel.

DISNEYLAND PARIS, 6:04 P.M.
Lights flicker on as daylight
fades, outlining the Victorian
buildings along Main Street,
U.S.A. The photograph was
taken from the Railroad Station.

OPPOSITE AND LEFT:
TOKYO DISNEYLAND, 2:07 P.M.
Bigger than life, the Carnivale Parade fills Main Street, U.S.A., with sound and color. A festive Minnie Mouse joins the Carnivale Parade festivities.

LEFT:
DISNEYLAND, CALIFORNIA, 9:09 P.M.
While it's Carnivale time in the afternoon in Tokyo Disneyland, the nighttime Mulan Parade makes its way down Main Street, U.S.A., in California.

LEFT:
DISNEYLAND, CALIFORNIA,
10:14 P.M.
Not long after the dancers in
Florida start winding down for the
night, swing dancers in Anaheim
are in high spirits at Fantasyland
Theater.

OPPOSITE:
TOKYO DISNEYLAND, 3:30 P.M.
Best friends posing at the Snow
White grotto in Fantasyland are
spending a memorable spring
day together.

10:00 P.M.   1:00 A.M.   7:00 A.M.   3:00 P.M.
CALIFORNIA   FLORIDA   PARIS   TOKYO

DISNEYLAND PARIS, 7:34 A.M.
A cast member polishes the rockets in Space
Mountain in preparation for the 9:00 A.M. opening.

DISNEYLAND, CALIFORNIA, 10:30 P.M.
The same attention to detail takes place in
California. Here a cast member adjusts the neon D
of the Disneyland Hotel logo, the same logo that
Walt Disney approved for the theme park in the
early 1950s.

LEFT:

WALT DISNEY WORLD, FLORIDA,
1:30 A.M.

In the wee hours of the morning, floats from the Main Street Electrical Parade line Main Street, U.S.A., in the Magic Kingdom for the taping of a television commercial announcing the arrival of the parade at the Florida park. After charming crowds in Disneyland, California since 1991, the captivating display of more than 700,000 twinkling bulbs is returning to the Magic Kingdom.

OPPOSITE:

TOKYO DISNEYLAND, 3:14 P.M.
Guests hop a ride on the Jolly Trolley, an off-kilter vehicle that jiggles, lurches, and weaves its way through Toontown.

WALT DISNEY WORLD, FLORIDA, 1:27 A.M.
Still wide awake and full of fun, the Pleasure Island
Dancers strike a pose for the photographer at
Mannequins dance club.

TOKYO DISNEYLAND, 3:32 P.M.
This youngster may be trying Pluto's patience by
pulling his tail, but 5-year-old Yosohiro Tsuzi can't
think of any other way to get the attention of his
favorite character.

WALT DISNEY WORLD, FLORIDA, 2:40 A.M.
After hours, real life interacts with almost real life as artist Carol Elferdink gives President Theodore Roosevelt a touch-up in the Hall of Presidents in the Magic Kingdom. Lifelike Audio-Animatronic® figures of all 42 chief executives fill the stage.

11:00 P.M.
CALIFORNIA

2:00 A.M.
FLORIDA

8:00 A.M.
PARIS

4:00 P.M.
TOKYO

TOKYO DISNEYLAND, 4:05 P.M.
A favorite school trip in Japan
is a day at Disneyland, where
kids can get very silly.

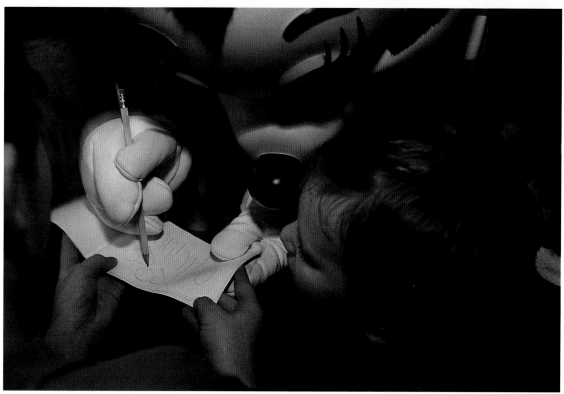

DISNEYLAND PARIS, 8:30 A.M.
This is as good as it gets—an
early-morning autograph and
a cozy little snuggle with
Minnie Mouse.

TOKYO DISNEYLAND, 4:13 P.M.
Youngsters can remove their shoes and leap into
Goofy's Bounce House in Toontown, which has bal-
loonlike furniture, walls, and floor.

DISNEYLAND PARIS, 8:02 A.M.
Gizzmo and Pépère enjoy
early-morning feeding time at
the Davy Crockett Ranch, the
campground at Disneyland
Paris, while two of the bisons
from Buffalo Bill's Wild West
Show start their day with a
breakfast of hay.

RIGHT:
DISNEYLAND, CALIFORNIA,
11:16 P.M.
The only snow-capped
mountain in Anaheim, the
famous Fantasyland
Matterhorn, is actually
built of wood and steel.
Dramatically lit after dark,
it remains one of the most
photogenic spots in the
park.

OPPOSITE:
TOKYO DISNEYLAND,
4:15 P.M.
Another mountain, another
continent, at another time
of day: the craggy land-
scape of Critter Country,
home to the Splash
Mountain clan.

Photo Credits

Alain Boniec   pages 33 (bottom), 36, 59, 70, 88-89, 89 (right), 102-103, 159 (top)

Scott Brinegar   pages 10, 16-17, 28, 32, 33 (top), 42 (bottom), 48, 55, 56, 61, 65, 66 (top), 78-79, 80, 82-83, 92, 93, 98, 105, 107, 116, 117, 123, 132-33, 140-41, 142, 145 (center), 147 (bottom), 148, 149, 152, 155 (bottom right), 156, 159 (bottom), 160, 161, 163 (bottom), 164-65, 166, 167, 168, 177 (bottom), 191

Jean-Claude Coutausse   pages 8 (bottom), 9 (both bottom), 11 (bottom left and bottom center), 24 (top), 25 (top), 29, 30, 31, 41, 44, 50, 51 (top left, center right, and center left), 53 (both right), 58, 60, 62 (top), 63, 66 (center and bottom), 67, 68, 69, 72, 73, 74 (bottom), 75, 84, 86-87, 90, 101 (bottom), 104, 114-15, 145 (bottom), 163 (top), 180, 187 (bottom), 189 (top)

Gene Duncan   pages 37, 42 (top), 45, 47, 49, 51 (top right), 57, 62 (bottom), 71, 109, 118, 121, 136, 137

Shigenobu Enami   pages 94, 111, 112, 125 (left), 153, 173 (bottom)

Youichirou Inatomi   pages 8-9 (top), 18 (top center), 25 (bottom), 26-27, 113, 128-29 (top), 144

Chieko Ishizawa   pages 15 (top), 21, 146 (bottom), 151 (top right), 164 (left), 188, 190

Marian Joseph   pages 74 (top), 91 (top)

Glen Miller   pages 178, 181

Eric Morency   pages 12, 13, 22, 40, 43, 46 (bottom), 76, 85, 97, 106, 114 (left), 120, 135, 173 (top), 174, 175, 189 (bottom)

Takeshi Obara   pages 11 (top), 15 (bottom), 18 (bottom left, bottom center, and bottom right, and top right and top left), 20, 23, 38, 52-53, 54, 126-27, 138, 139, 157, 176, 177 (top), 183

David Roark   pages 3, 11 (bottom right), 34-35 (top), 39, 102 (top), 108, 119, 128-29 (bottom), 182, 186

Katsuhiro Tsukada   pages 14, 19, 46 (top), 77, 81, 95, 96, 101 (top), 125 (right), 130, 143, 146 (top), 147 (top), 162, 172, 179, 185, 187 (top)

Molly VanWagner   pages 64, 91 (bottom), 124, 126 (left), 131, 145 (top), 150, 151

Garth Vaughan   pages 24 (bottom), 35 (bottom), 51 (bottom left and bottom right), 134, 154-55, 158, 169, 170, 171, 184

David Valdez   pages 79 (right), 86 (left), 99, 100, 110, 122